Martin de Porres

A Beggar for Justice

1579–1639

Born in Lima, Peru

Feast Day: November 3

Patronage:

Social justice

Text by Barbara Yoffie
Illustrated by Katherine A. Borgatti

Liguori

Dedication

To my family:
my parents Jim and Peg,
my husband Bill,
our son Sam and daughter-in-law Erin,
and our precious grandchildren
Ben, Lucas, and Andrew

To all the children I have had the privilege of teaching throughout the years.

Imprimi Potest:
Harry Grile, CSsR, Provincial
Denver Province, The Redemptorists

Published by Liguori Publications
Liguori, Missouri 63057

To order, call 800-325-9521
Liguori.org

p ISBN: 978-0-7648-2329-9
e ISBN: 978-0-7648-6849-8

Liguori Publications, a nonprofit corporation, is an apostolate of The Redemptorists. To learn more about The Redemptorists, visit Redemptorists.com.

Printed in the United States of America
23 22 21 20 19 / 6 5 4 3 2
First Edition

Dear Parents and Teachers:

Saints and Me! is a series of children's books about saints, with six books in each set. The first set is titled *Saints of North America*. This second set, *Saints of Christmas,* selects seven heavenly heroes who teach us to love the Infant Jesus. Some saints in this set have feast days within Advent and Christmas time, but others are celebrated within ordinary time and Easter time. We selected these saints based on their connection to the Christmas story and how they inspire us to let the mystery of Christ's birth grow within our hearts.

Saints of Christmas includes the heroic lives of seven saints from different times and places who loved Jesus. Saints Mary and Joseph witnessed the miracle of God's abundant love for humanity as our Infant Savior entered the world to bring us home to God. Saint Lucy followed Jesus in a time when Christianity was against the law. The story of Saint Nicholas was so incredible that it inspired our secular notion of Santa Claus. Saint Francis of Assisi added much flavor to our current Christmas traditions. Saint Martin de Porres is a biracial saint who teaches us about divine love for all people. And a saint of our own era, Gianna Beretta Molla, witnessed a deep belief in the gift of life.

Which saint cared for slaves from Africa? Who became a doctor and mother? What saints were present at Jesus' birth in Bethlehem? Who desired to be a knight? Which saint was a bishop of a seaport city? Do you know which saint's name means "light?" Find the answers in the *Saints of Christmas* set, part of the *Saints and Me!* series, and help your child identify with the lives of the saints.

Introduce your children or students to the *Saints and Me!* series as they:

—**READ** about the lives of the saints and are inspired by their stories.

—**PRAY** to the saints for their intercession.

—**CELEBRATE** the saints and relate to their lives.

saints of Christmas

advent	week 1			
	week 2			
	week 3			
	week 4			
christmas	week 5			
	week 6			

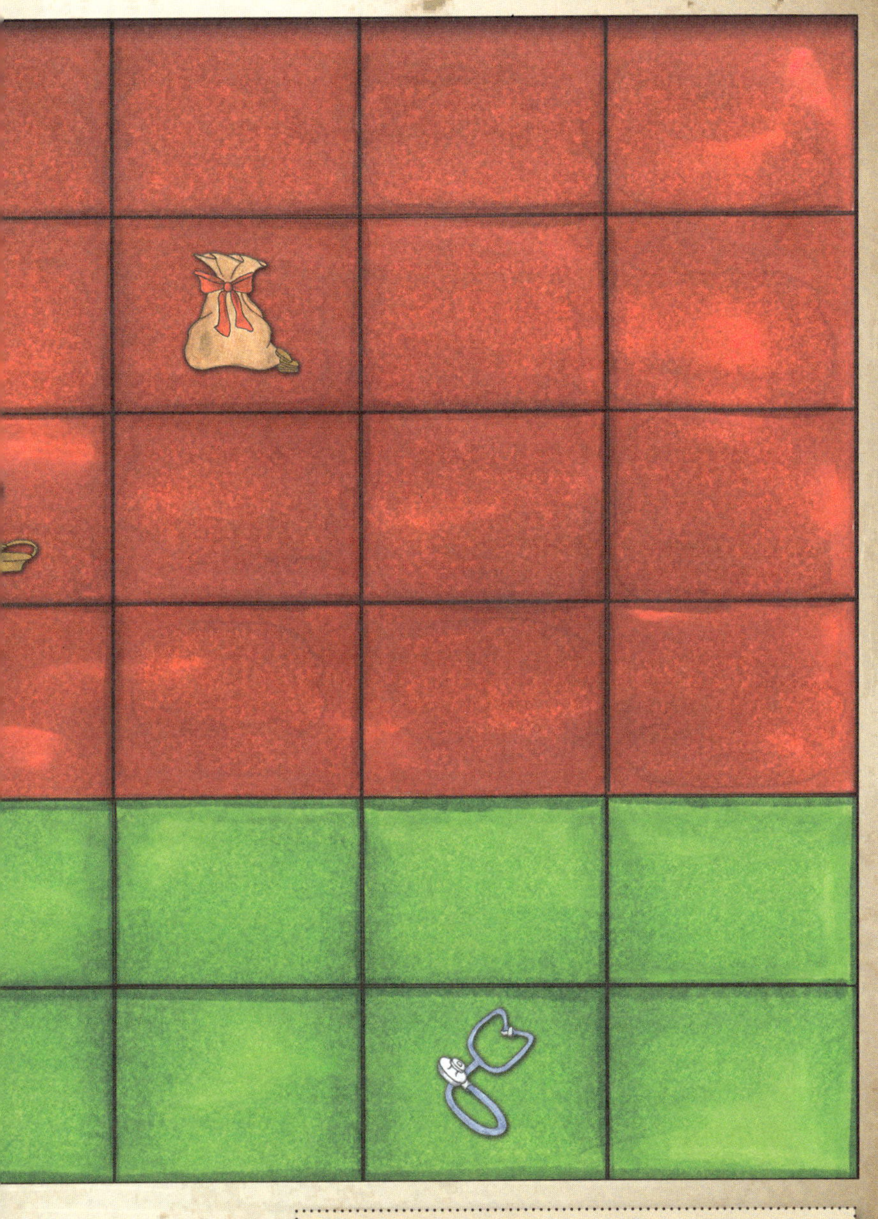

Mary and Joseph

Lucy

Nicholas of Myra

Francis of Assisi

Martin de Porres

Gianna Beretta Molla

This is a story about a very kind boy named Martin de Porres. He lived in Peru, a country in South America. Little Martin had brown eyes and dark skin just like his mother.

His father, a Spanish soldier, moved away when Martin was young. Life was not easy for Martin. Children laughed at him because of his dark skin. He did not have lots of toys and clothes. Sometimes he went to bed hungry.

But instead of being sad, Martin was cheerful. And instead of being mad at people, he was helpful and kind. He prayed every day. Martin loved God with all his heart.

One day Martin's mother sent him to the market. He bought bread and potatoes. Martin put the food in his basket and began to run home. When he saw a beggar on the side of the road, he stopped. The beggar looked hungry. "Here, take this," Martin said with a smile. He gave all his food to the poor woman.

When Martin was only twelve years old he worked with a doctor. Martin learned how to make medicine from herbs. He learned how to help people with fevers, rashes, and broken bones. Helping sick people made Martin very happy.

Praying also made Martin very happy. He liked going to church. He loved God very much. Martin joined the Dominican order as a lay helper. Lay helpers are not priests; they serve God in other ways.

Martin was a hard worker and had many jobs at the monastery. He swept the floors, fed the animals, and worked in the garden. Each day was filled with work and prayer.

The Dominican brothers saw that Martin was holy and good. "Martin, we want you to become a brother." So Martin made his vows and was called Brother Martin.

Brother Martin worked in the infirmary at the monastery. An infirmary is a small hospital. He talked to each patient: “Good morning. How are you feeling today?” Then he would pray with them. Brother Martin helped people feel better.

Brother Martin opened an orphanage and a hospital. He gave out food and supplies to people in the city. He cared for the slaves from Africa. When the Dominican order needed money, Brother Martin would beg in the streets.

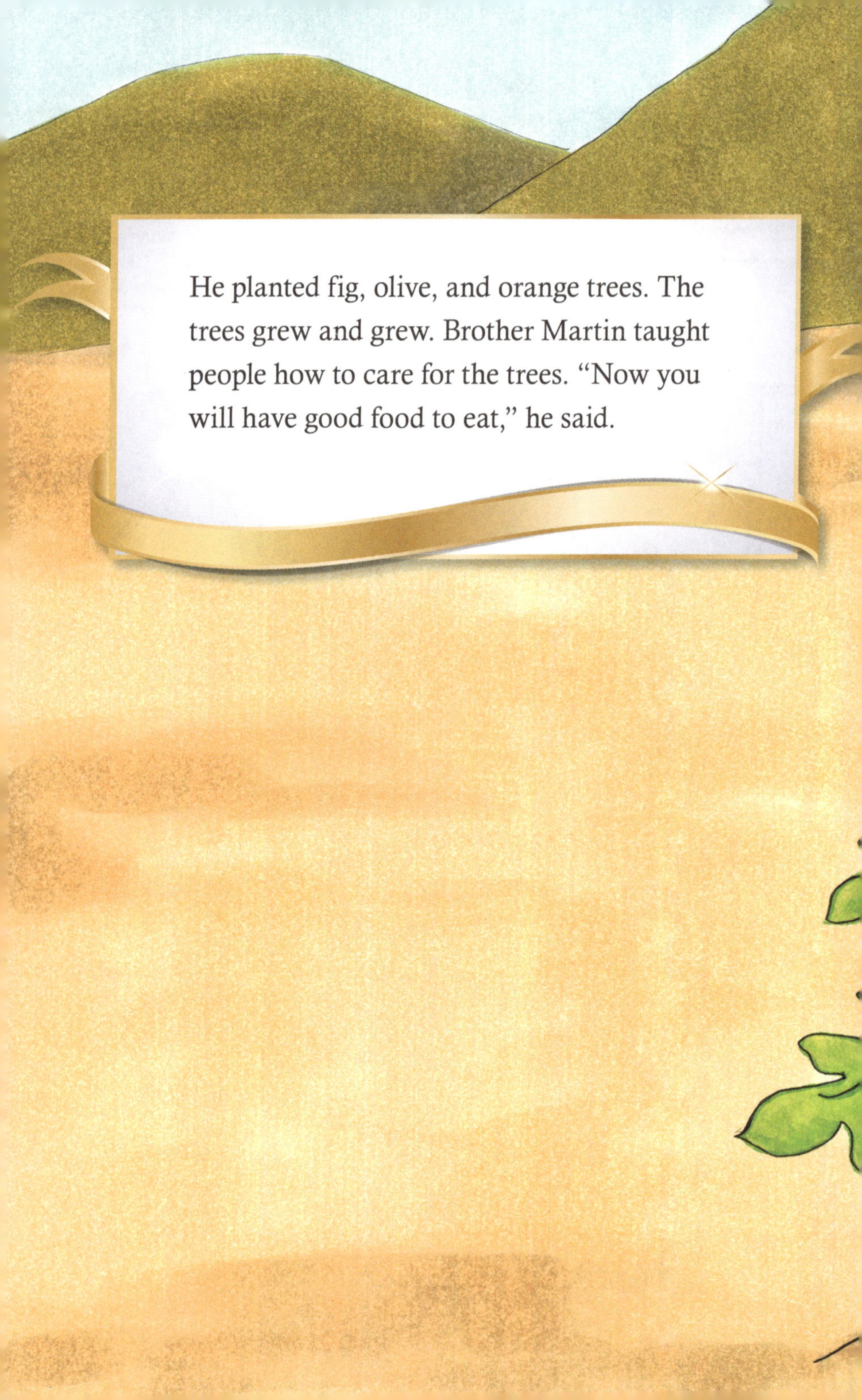

He planted fig, olive, and orange trees. The trees grew and grew. Brother Martin taught people how to care for the trees. "Now you will have good food to eat," he said.

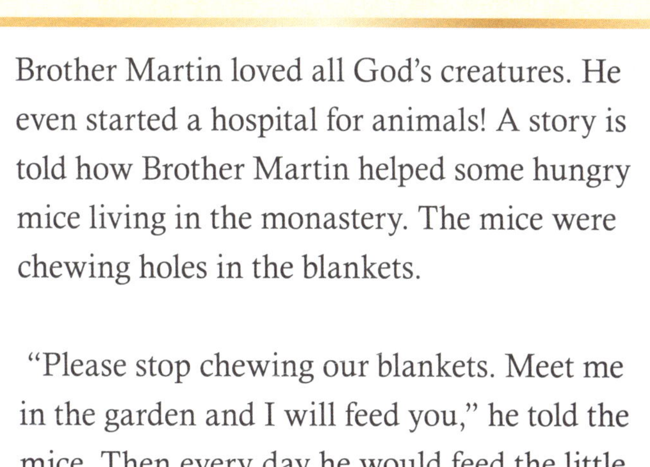

Brother Martin loved all God's creatures. He even started a hospital for animals! A story is told how Brother Martin helped some hungry mice living in the monastery. The mice were chewing holes in the blankets.

"Please stop chewing our blankets. Meet me in the garden and I will feed you," he told the mice. Then every day he would feed the little creatures. And the mice did not return to the monastery.

Everyone loved Brother Martin. His heart was full of love for all people and all races. He felt that they were his brothers and sisters.

One day Brother Martin got very sick. He had a high fever and was very tired. The Dominican brothers came to his room to pray with him. He told them, "I will pray for you in heaven." They cried when he died.

Many important people came to Brother Martin's funeral. They wanted to say good-bye to this holy and kind man. They called him "Martin of Charity." His whole life had been a gift to others.

Brother Martin believed in helping others.
All people are our sisters and brothers.

INRI

Dear God,

I love you.

Saint Martin de Porres

loved you, too.

He loved all people

and was very kind.

Help me to be loving

and kind.

Amen.

NEW WORDS (Glossary)

Beggar: Someone who asks for food or money

Brother: A male member of a religious order who takes special vows

Charity: Another word for "love," an action we show toward God and neighbor

Dominican order: A religious community founded by Saint Dominic in 1216

Herb: A plant used as medicine or to flavor food

Infirmary: A small hospital

Lay helper: One who helps at or works for a religious order

Monastery: The place where a religious order lives, prays, and works

Orphanage: A home for children who do not have parents

Social justice: Working together to help all people live with dignity

Vow: A special promise made to God

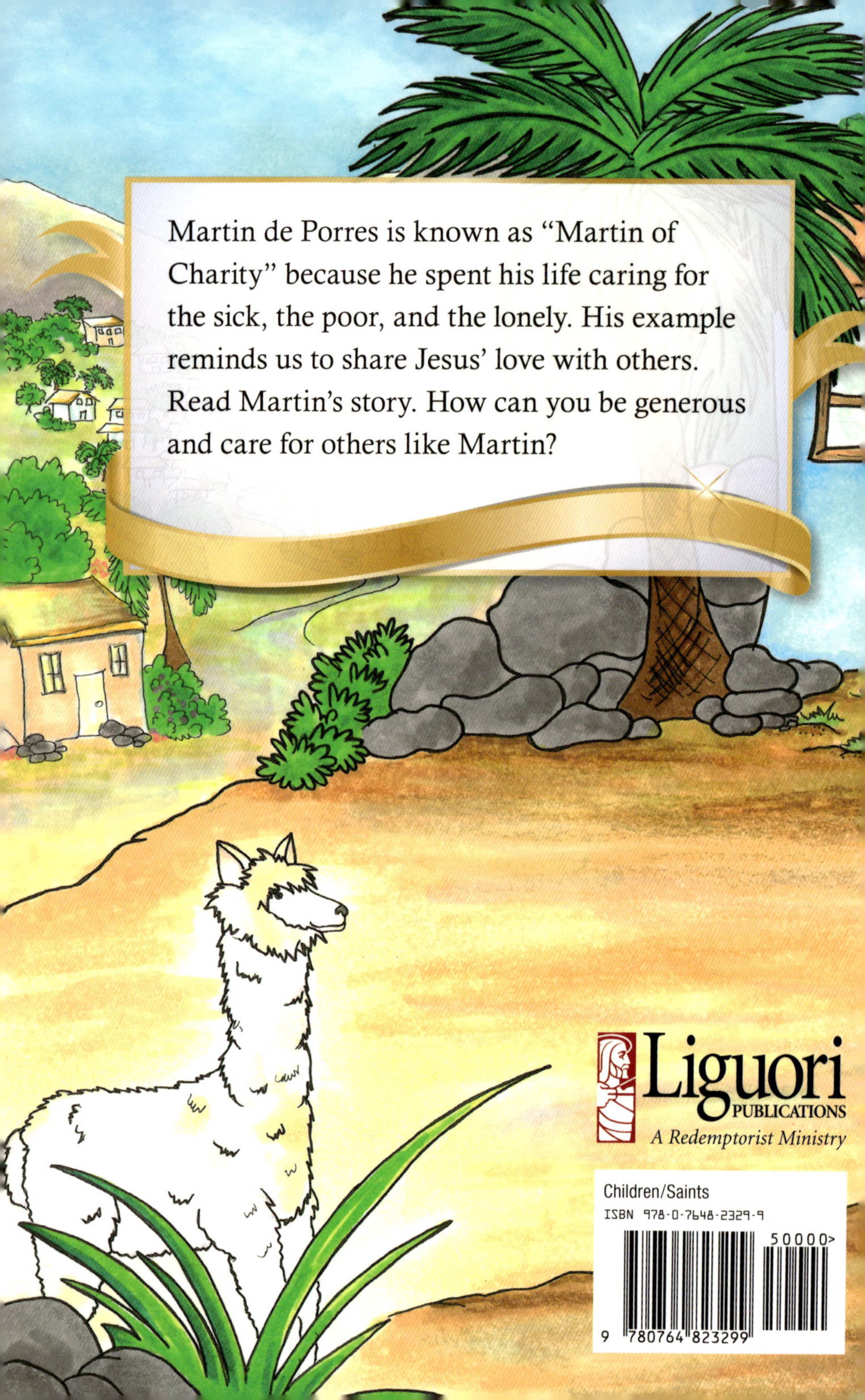

Martin de Porres is known as "Martin of Charity" because he spent his life caring for the sick, the poor, and the lonely. His example reminds us to share Jesus' love with others. Read Martin's story. How can you be generous and care for others like Martin?

Liguori PUBLICATIONS
A Redemptorist Ministry

Children/Saints
ISBN 978-0-7648-2329-9
50000>
9 780764 823299

Padre Pio

Saint for Reconciliation

Barbara Yoffie

Illustrated by Jeff Albrecht